LECTURES ON REVIVAL
FOR
A LAODICEAN CHURCH

E. A. JOHNSTON

ISBN: 979-8-9896619-2-3

Printed in the United States of America
January 2024

Formatting and Publishing by
The Old Paths Publications, Inc
4439 Rockrose Green Way
Gainesville, GA 30504
TOP@theoldpathspublications.com
www.theoldpathspublications.com

COVER PHOTOS:

E. A. Johnston in various pulpits

The first image on the left is Wesley's New Room in Bristol, England. The middle image is the pulpit of St. Mary de Crypt, Gloucester, England, from which George Whitefield preached his first sermon and 15 people made professions of faith. The third image is Whitefield's outdoor pulpit in England.

DEDICATION

The following chapters on the study of revival are dedicated with warm esteem to a man whom God raised up to republish my written works in a day of spiritual declension, to whom I am very grateful: DR. H. D. WILLIAMS, Publisher Old Paths Publications.

E. A. Johnston
January 2024

TABLE OF CONTENTS

PREFACE

Desperate times call for desperate prayer but who is desperate enough to pray desperately? As society spins out of control into moral chaos, the church lies in a deep spiritual stupor unaware of the encroaching danger around her, much like Jonah asleep in the side of the ship in the midst of the storm.

What cataclysmic events must occur to get the people of God's attention? If tragedy and calamity do not drive us to our knees in prayer, what will?

This book is a call to our knees. A call to revival. It is a call to a return to vital Apostolic Christianity, where Christ is once again preeminent in the church and prominent in the life and a power of God in our meetings.

E. A. Johnston

CHAPTER ONE
DARK TIMES

"John Wesley and George Whitefield stood out like two brilliant diamonds against the dark velvet backdrop of a degenerate Age and an apostate church, mainly comprised of an unconverted ministry."

E. A. Johnston

We look around us today and wonder at the darkness of our times—where perversion permeates the very fabric of society and the Church lies impotent as an outdated institution. The Nation lies under the remedial judgments of God (Amos chapter four) where calamity and natural disasters increase with great severity. We turn on the news and see reports of floods, fires, earthquakes, hurricanes and disasters and it reads like a page from the Old Testament. Almighty God through His remedial judgments is displaying mercy to draw us back to Him. But yet, we do not heed the warnings nor even recognize them as Divine displeasure against us! Blindly, we press on and sin more and more and fill our cup of iniquity as a nation until our destruction is a reality—and America and England, once two great nations for God lie in the ash heap of ruined civilizations like ancient Rome and ancient Greece.

Sadly, at a time when society and the church need revival the most, they are least interested in returning to the God of the Bible. There is no fear of God in the land and no fear of God in the church. Antinomianism is rampant in our congregations and holiness is a taboo subject!

We preach a man-centered Gospel focused on the happiness and satisfaction of man. We have shrunken God down to man's size and taken salvation out of the hands of God and placed it in the hands of men. We get saved when we are good and ready by a decision we make, rather than the regenerating Spirit of God. Most so-called believers today sit on the rotten foundation of a empty religious profession that was still-birthed by easy believeism. Ninety percent of our congregations are yet unregenerate individuals with no reality of God in the life.

Our pulpits are occupied mainly by entertainers or CEO's who know how to run a corporation but they don't know God. In our pulpits stand teachers and not preachers, who either just dish out information or funny stories, or read a Bible passage with a fill-in-the blank teaching methodology. We desire to keep our congregations busy and occupied during the service but there is no spiritual depth or transformation of the life. So we meet each Sunday for fellowship, sing a few upbeat songs while we clap our hands and sway our hips and we listen to non-expository message and we hand in our envelope with our tithe and we call that Christianity. Meanwhile, the world perishes and Hell fills up by the minute! Jesus never meant for us to build large buildings for our own creature comforts to present a "come and hear message" rather, His was a "go and tell Gospel" of the Great Commission. Your average so-called Christian today has no personal witness in their community—they don't even witness to their lost loved ones or neighbors. Like I already stated, our times are a very dark time and time is running out!

CHAPTER TWO
REALIZING OUR NEED FOR REVIVAL

"In 1740 when God moved through New England it was called 'The Great Awakening.' Revival has often been referred to as 'an awakening.' At Gethsemane, Jesus faced the 'crisis point' of His earthly ministry and His disciples slept right through it. Today the church is in a 'crises point' and we are sleeping right through it."

E. A. Johnston

In the book of Hosea there is an interesting comparison of the backslidden Jews to an unbaked cake. We read in Hosea, chapter seven and in verses eight and nine: "Ephraim, he hath mixed himself among the people; Ephraim is a cake not turned." Meaning it is half-baked; done only on one side. The side that is visible appears to be presentable for nourishment but underneath it is uncooked and inedible! The Jews in the days of Hosea were enjoying a period of peace and material prosperity under the reign of King Jeroboam II of Israel. But despite their outward prosperity they were spiritually bankrupt and so backslidden they were completely unaware of their spiritual decay. God tells them,

> *"Strangers have devoured his strength, and he knoweth not: yea, gray hairs are here and there upon him, yet he knoweth not" (Hosea 7:9).*

And God laments in chapter eleven,

> *"And my people are bent to backsliding from me."*

Today, the modern church is backslidden and completely unaware of her condition! We have a perfect picture of this from the Book of Revelation concerning the Laodicean Church. Jesus tells them,

> *"I know thy works, that thou art neither cold nor hot: I would thou wast cold or hot. So then because thou art lukewarm, and neither cold nor hot, I will spew thee out of my mouth. Because*

thou sayest, I am rich, and increased with goods, and have need of nothing, and knowest not that thou art wretched, and miserable, and poor, and blind, and naked" (Revelation 3:15-17).

A self-satisfied, self-reliant people are distasteful to a thrice holy God! There was a time long ago, when the church had power and influence in the land because the people of God relied entirely upon God in their daily living and service to Him. But the modern church figured out that we can get things done faster with money and manpower—but the church in former days operated on prayer and Holy Ghost power! Only a heaven sent revival can awaken us to our desperate and deplorable condition!

I was talking to Iain Murray, who was ninety-two at the time, about revival and I asked him the following question: "What do you feel is the greatest need for revival today?" He chuckled and replied, "Well, that's a pretty good question, isn't it?" and then he said, "First, we must appreciate the need for revival, and then believe what God can do to bring revival about; and to know our dependency is entirely upon Him." I thought that was an excellent answer. The church at this hour must recognize the NEED for revival. We must exercise the faith and grace to believe a Sovereign God will send us revival. We must not rely on fleshly efforts to bring it about but we can prepare our hearts while we wait upon Him. A good illustration of this is what my homiletical mentor Dr. Stephen F. Olford described about revival, he said,

"I am forcefully reminded of an expository sermon on revival I heard from the lips of the great Dr. G. Campbell Morgan during my theological studies in London, England—many years ago! What the doctor had to say has helped me to understand how God and man come together in his holy business of praying down revival from heaven.

"Let me paraphrase what I heard and remember. Revival is a sovereign work of God. Jesus declared, 'The wind blows where it wishes, and you hear the sound of it, but cannot tell where it comes from and where it goes.

So is everyone who is born (or revived) of the Spirit' (John 3:8).

"Only God can command the revival wind. But, we must set our sails to catch the wind when GOD BLOWS! There you have it: we cannot produce revival, but we can ready ourselves to receive it when it comes."

When sleepy-headed pastors wake up to realize the need for revival, then and only then, will they pray aright and call their people to gather together to seek the Lord of glory to rain His righteousness down upon them in plentiful effusions of His grace!

CHAPTER THREE
REALIZING OUR SPIRITUAL DECAY

"When we are not exercising our graces we are slumbering in spiritual decay. Had Noah exercised his graces more than guzzling his grapes, he would not have lain naked in his tent sleeping off his hangover. Had Lot been exercising his graces more than worrying about his skin, he would have been more aware to the depravity of his daughters. Had David been exercising his graces by leading a battle for God rather than reclining on his couch he would have avoided the nakedness of Bathsheba and following the lustful inclinations of his heart."

E. A. Johnston

When the people of God fail to exercise their graces and fear God and serve Him with their whole heart, then they fall into the most grievous and aggravated sins against the Almighty without any concern for anyone but themselves and their own sinful gratification. The church today is ripe with antinomianism from the pulpit to the pew. The prevailing philosophy in our churches seems to be "once saved always saved, therefore I can sin all I want to and still go to heaven."

Holiness is a taboo subject in our pulpits today and many churches have fallen into compromise and conformity to the evil society in which they exist. When churches relax and recline rather than kneel and intercede we lose our power with God and our witness to the world. Instead of being on our knees and in our Bibles we are on our couches watching tv. We are full of the world instead of being full of the Spirit. The first step back to God is repentance; God declares: *"Return unto me, and I will return unto you, saith the LORD of hosts"* (Malachi 3:7). The first step toward revival is to be honest with ourselves in regard to our own spiritual condition and realize our spiritual decay. If we fail to realize our spiritual decay we will not recognize the need for revival! When the people of God realize their spiritual decay they will awaken out of their spiritual stupor and proclaim with Ephraim,

"What have I to do any more with idols" (Hosea 14:8)?

The first thing lacking in a people who are in spiritual decay and backsliding is no fear of God. In the modern church we have shrunken God down to our size today and view God as a man who acts as we do and behaves as we do. God gave the prophet Jeremiah a message to His backslidden people; in Jeremiah chapter five and verses 20-25 we read:

> *"Declares this in the house of Jacob, and publish it in Judah, saying, Hear now this, O foolish people, and without understanding; which have eyes, and see not; which have ears, and hear not: Fear ye not me? saith the LORD: will ye not tremble at my presence, which have placed the sand for the bound of the sea by a perpetual decree, that it cannot pass it: and though the waves thereof toss themselves, yet can they not prevail; though they roar, yet they not pass over it? But this people hath a*

revolting and a rebellious heart; they are revolted and gone. Neither say they in their heart, Let us not fear the LORD our God, that giveth rain, both the former and the latter in his season: he reserveth unto us the appointed weeks of the harvest. Your iniquities have turned away these things, and your sins have withholden good things for you."

A spiritually decayed church needs revival. A spiritually decayed people need revival. A spiritually decayed Nation needs revival! There is no fear of God in the land today: neither in society or in the pulpits of our land. Instead of flourishing, the church is languishing. She has become merely an institution without any power. We are living under the remedial judgement of God by His withdrawn presence from among us. When was the last time you felt the power of God in a meeting? When was the last time the Holy Spirit convicted you of sin? When was the last time you spent the evening out of bed and on your knees crying out to God in desperate prayer? When the people of God are not exercising their graces then they are abusing the grace God has given them and trampling the Blood of the Son by presumptuous sin.

The shortest definition of sin found in my Bible is in Isaiah chapter fifty three and verse six, which states: *"All we like sheep have gone astray; we have turned every one to his own way..."*

Sin is going "our way" when we know it isn't "God's way!"

A fear of God will keep us from sin. A fear of God will prevent us from falling into spiritual decay, as a people and as a Nation.

CHAPTER FOUR
ABSENCE: AUTHORITY AND POWER

"There can be only one answer to the question, 'Why has the Church lost her power?' The answer lies in the reality that the Church has forsaken the Third Person of the Trinity, replacing Him with programs, money and man-centered methodologies. Our reliance is one of self, rather reliance upon the Holy Spirit to empower us to pray, preach, and witness with an enduement from on High."

E. A. Johnston

The missing element in our churches today is the Holy Spirit. There is an absence of His authority and power. Without the Holy Spirit present in our midst we will not fall under conviction of sin. Jesus said of the Spirit: *"And when he is come, he will reprove the world of sin, and of righteousness, and of judgment"* (John 16:8). And Jesus told His disciples to wait upon the Spirit for power and anointing:

"And, behold, I send the promise of my Father upon you: but tarry ye in the city of Jerusalem, until ye be endued with power from on high" (Luke 24:49).

This enduement of the Holy Spirit is the missing element in our pulpits today. The anointing of the Spirit is unknown in many churches in our land. How can blind eyes be opened? How can deaf ears hear? How can dead men rise? If not the Spirit of God attends the preaching of His holy Word! I was struck by the following observation of the Puritan Thomas Goodwin:

"Thomas Goodwin, after hearing Rogers of Dedham preach, hung 'a quarter of an hour upon the neck of his horse weeping, before he had power to mount.'"

I think of that man hanging onto his horse's mane, his tears staining the ground below him, unable to move because the power of God was manifest in the preaching and the Spirit of God wrought a work of conviction in his heart! That is what we need today in our churches! That is what we need today in our preaching! That is what we need today in our praying! That is what we need today in our witnessing! Not our strength and ability—but the power of God by His Spirit. We read in Zechariah 4:6, *"Then he answered and spake unto me, saying, This is the word of the LORD unto Zerubbabel, saying, Not by might, nor by power, but by my Spirit saith the LORD of hosts."*

In times of revival a revived church will have power and authority and influence in the community. Instead of Satan gaining ground on every corner, the darkness will not prevail but be pushed back by an ignited church!

I was having lunch with a pastor from Glasgow, Scotland and he related to me the following story. He said, that his city of Glasgow used to have a city banner that was written all around the city and it had been that way for over two hundred years. The Banner was the slogan for the city of Glasgow and it read: "Let Glasgow flourish in the name of the Lord and in His power!" But some ungodly civic leaders voted to remove that banner from the city of Glasgow and replace it with only the words, "Let Glasgow Flourish!" The new city slogan was purely humanistic. And this pastor from Glasgow told me that as soon as the city removed the old banner and replaced it, that crime and evil began to grow in his city. There was a noticeable increase in drugs, crime, and unwanted pregnancies. Soon things were growing more and more evil every day as Satan expanded his territory. Then this godly pastor became so overwrought by the increase of evil and sin in his community that he banded together with four other pastors to pray weekly for a godly return to Glasgow. He told me that after several months of serious intercession these men began to see a noticeable decrease in crime and evil and unwanted pregnancies. By their faith and prayers they had PUSHED BACK THE DARKNESS within their community! If the Church is not fulfilling her mandate of the Great Commission and being a Light living for God in the world then a vacuum is created that is filled with darkness.

The anointing of the Holy Spirit comes with a price because anything worthwhile like higher education, learning a trade, or waiting upon God has a cost. What costs counts and what counts costs! There are conditions associated with the anointing of the Spirit. My homiletical mentor, Dr. Stephen F. Olford taught that "The Anointing of the Spirit" had certain conditions which are:

1. Holiness
2. Yieldedness
3. Prayerfulness.

CHAPTER FIVE
PRAYING FOR REVIVAL

"God will always raise up an Elijah whose prayers impact a sleeping nation. The Church in each generation has had individuals who live on their knees, whose prayers reach heaven with a holy violence. India had her 'Praying Hyde'; China her John Sung; England her Puritans; Scotland her Covenanters; America her fiery E. M. Bounds. Voices which gained the attention of the Throne-room, startled angels, and shook the gates of hell, making even the demons quake and tremble with their desperate prayers."

E. A. Johnston

Intercessory prayer is a lost art today. Even many in our churches today do not know how to pray corporately. When the churches killed off the weekly prayer meeting and replaced it with divorce recovery groups and Rumba classes we lost the only power we had.

There is a story about Charles Spurgeon, the great British preacher. One day he was entertaining a visitor to his church, a young man fresh out of seminary. Spurgeon asked the young man if he would like to see the engine of the church. The young man nodded his head. Spurgeon led the man down a stairwell to the basement, where the young man assumed that he was to be shown the boiler room of the church, but instead, Spurgeon led the young man to a set of double doors in the basement which upon opening revealed three hundred deacons on their knees in prayer! And the great preacher commented: "Here my good man is the engine of my church!"

If prayer is the engine of the church then that explains why so many churches are out of gas! The modern church has figured out that they can get more done today with money and manpower, but the church in former times operated solely on God and Holy Ghost power! But sadly, few pastors today spend much time engaged in the activity of prayer. Dr. Stephen Olford shared with me that the average pastor only spent ten minutes in prayer each day. Ten minutes! If that is true then what does the average believer spend in prayer each day? Two minutes? Perhaps three? As they merely pray, "God bless me, and mine. Amen."

When one studies historical revival it is soon learned that most revivals began with prayer. Things were so bad in England during the days of Wesley and Whitefield that every fifth house in London was a gin shop, and public drunkenness was a plague to society—even members of Parliament showed up for work "dead drunk". It was during long nights of prayer in the Holy Club at Oxford where a young George Whitefield met weekly with John and Charles Wesley and other students who were serious about religion to read the Bible, recite hymns, and pray and fast entire nights for the nation. This group of young dedicated men were soon labeled "The Methodists" because of their method of diligent religious activity and rigorous lives of self-denial. The revival of religion under John Wesley and George Whitefield in England was birthed by prayer.

In America, during the Second Great Awakening there was a great revival of religion taking place across the land. Men like Charles Finney and Daniel Nash would pray entire nights and days for God to save a community. Father Nash (as Finney called him) would enter a city weeks before Charles Finney arrived to preach to saturate the city in ceaseless prayer. Back then when God was moving in the land in spiritual awakening it was common for Christians to pray several hours at a time. Now in our churches we merely tip our hat to God because we don't have time to pray and this is why there is so much deadness and dryness and apathy and indifference in our churches across the land.

John Sung, whom God used to shake China in revival, was a man of prayer. His daughter Levi tells us in her biography of her father,

> "He would kneel and pray every night, even after a long and grueling day. During his period of convalescence at Fragrant Hills, he would pray on his knees for hours after Bible study sessions with fellow workers. Five hours at a stretch were not too long for him…he would kneel on one

knee when he found his wounds too painful to do so on both."[1]

Sam Jones, the great evangelist of the late 19th century, was a man of prayer and prayer was the springboard to his many revivals. One incident in his life bears mention in regard to prayer and revival because after he spent the night in prayer an entire town was saved! We see from the following narrative:

> "At Tuscumbia, Alabama, he held a large bush-arbor meeting. Three and four services were held daily, and people came in from all parts of the country. Some of the most remarkable manifestations of the presence of God were seen in that arbor meeting. The people marveled at the results, and perhaps the secret was not known to them; however, it can be attributed to the earnest prayers of Mr. Jones. The great audiences that he preached to did not know how

---

[1] Levi, "The Journal Once Lost" Diary of John Sung. (Singapore: Genesis Books, 2008) p 27.

many times he wrestled with God in prayer before preaching. Just before the greatest manifestation of the Spirit's work, Mr. Jones had been very earnest in prayer. He was always a man who went to the throne of mercy for the anointing of service…there was a great crises in the meeting, and he met it by a long season of prayer.

"The people had made all kinds of threats against him, so after the night service he walked onto the second story of the porch and knelt down in a corner, the thick vines almost hiding him. He remained there until midnight, and yet no assurance of victory. The morning hours came, and he was still on his knees. He had not undressed or been asleep that night. The great audience assembled for the six o'clock (am) service; perhaps there were twenty-five hundred present. He arose to preach, and such power came upon the people that the town was won to God."[2]

Revivals are bathed and birthed in prayer. We must pray with the psalmist: *"Thy people shall be willing in the day of thy power"* (Psalm 110:3). We shall speak about what revival is in the next chapter.

---

[2] E. A. Johnston, "Sam Jones A New Biography" (Georgia: Old Paths Publications, 2023). Pp 190-191.

CHAPTER SIX
WHAT IS REVIVAL?

"He was called 'The Wonder of the Ages' and 'The Sledgehammer.' Listening to Sam Jones preach was both an enjoyable and painful experience; enjoyable because he got you to laugh about yourself and others, painful because his sledgehammer preaching unearthed all the vermin hidden for years beneath a false foundation of self-righteousness and fabricated veneer of self-delusion."

E. A. Johnston

A revival is not a series of evangelistic meetings, with loud music, loud singing, loud praying, and loud preaching. That is something the church does for the community. A revival is a sovereign work of God that He performs for His church. In a revival there will be a power of God in the meeting and the manifest presence of the Almighty.

Revival is when the spiritual vitality of the people of God is ignited by the Spirit of God and Christ once again is preeminent in the sanctuary and prominent in the life of a believer. I will describe revival as I have personally witnessed it in my own life and ministry.

In the early 1990's I began to have a real hunger for revival. I was a Sunday school teacher in a large Baptist church in the South and I started a men's discipleship group in my home with met on Tuesday evenings at 6:30pm. I ended up having about twelve to fifteen men attend this weekly discipleship group. I prayed about what to teach them and decided on taking them through Charles Finney's book *"Lectures On Revival."* Our church bookstore carried the book and I had the men each buy their own copy and we began each week to go thru Finney's book on revival. I would start the meeting with a time of prayer then I would hand each man a bible verse to memorize that particular week. We would share prayer requests with one another as we sat in a circle in my living room.

As we went deeper into Finney's book, God began to deal with the men in the group. Lives were being changed for the glory of God.

It was not uncommon for me to get a phone call in the middle of the night from a worried wife who begged me to drive over to their home to pray with her distressed husband. And when I arrived there I saw a man crumpled on the floor by his easy chair, his face bathed in tears and his person anxious. That time of discipling that group of men demonstrated to me the reality that God gets serious with those who get serious with Him!

I began to get serious with God and He got serious with me. I began to meet in the chapel at my church, three mornings a week from 6:30am to 7:30am to meet with another believer to pray for revival to come to our church and community. We did this for a period of six months without seeing revival visit our church. However, God led us to another church in a nearby State that was experiencing a real revival. This was my first introduction to a real move of God in a church revival.

The out-of-town church was a hour and a half away and by the time me and another man arrived there we were late. It was a Saturday evening service and the church sanctuary sat 1,000 and as we entered the church we realized we were arriving at the middle or end of the service. The place was packed. There were only two vacant seats up in the balcony and my friend and I took our seats and tried to understand what was transpiring before us. The place was as a quiet as a library and there was no pastor on the platform—the platform was vacant, except for two rows of choir members who silently passed a Kleenex box around to wipe their tears.

Suddenly I felt an incredible urge to cry. I could not explain it but tears began to roll down my cheeks. I slowly turned my head to look at my friend and big tears were dripping off his chin. What was going on? I wondered. Then I felt the awful solemnity of a Holy God before me. it was the manifest presence of the Almighty and I realized that was the reason for my tears. I was faced with His holiness! And I was a sinner! As we glanced out at the church members seated around the sanctuary we realized that 1,000 people were silently weeping before the Lord.

After about two hours of that silent worship the meeting ended and people began to disperse to go home. It was dark outside and 10:30pm as we made our way through the church parking lot. I noticed a man slowly walking to his car and I recognized him as the pastor of the church and we approached him.

I said, "Can you tell me what's going on around here?" He looked beat and worn out, but he answered me by saying, "I had a message to preach tonight but I never got around to it. The Holy Spirit showed up and took control and I sat down." Then he turned to go to his car. I ran up beside him and grabbed his arm and said, "We drove an hour and a half to get here, can't you tell me any more than that?" He looked me in the eye and said, "All I can tell you is we are dead people." And with that he got in his truck and drove off. My friend and I stood beneath a moonlit night in a church parking lot in Mississippi scratching our heads.

That Monday I telephoned the church secretary to see if she could be more specific about the revival taking place. She took the time to explain to me what was going on. It seems the men of the church attended a men's retreat two weekends ago, conducted by a missionary from Africa. During that men's retreat some of the men gave their hearts to God in a serious surrender to Him. Those men went home to their families and the wives noticed an immediate change in their husbands. Their husbands were changed men—they spoke softly and sweetly to their wives and held their hands as they prayed with them each morning before they left for work. They quickly became the spiritual leaders in the home leading the family in the ways of the Lord. Soon, the wives of these men were so overwhelmed and grateful to God for the change in their husbands and life of the family that the women of the church went forward one night and dedicated their lives to God in a fresh surrender. Soon the teenagers in the home saw what it was like to have two godly parents with the reality of God in their daily living that one night at church the teenagers broke down and came forward and surrendered their lives to Christ! This was the night that my friend and I were in attendance, we had arrived too late and we missed all that taking place—what we came into was the thankfulness of the parents, weeping before the Lord for the salvation of their teenagers!

That is what revival can do to the life of a church! When God shows up and the people of God become transparent and broken before Him in humility and contriteness and repentance. That was my introduction to revival and I believe God allowed me to witness it because of my six months of serious prayer for revival. Like I said, God gets serious with us when we get serious with Him!

Once God called me to be His preacher and I began preaching I saw revival first hand on several occasions. I was preaching at the Stephen Olford Center in Memphis, Tennessee on a Wednesday evening for pastors. And I took with me two of the men I was discipling at the time and I gave them strict instructions. They were to sit at the back of the room and the entire time I was preaching they were to be praying. Finney had his Father Nash and Able Clary and that night I had my two praying friends! I was preaching out of the fifteenth chapter of the Gospel of John on the Vine and the branches. And I mentioned to the twenty or so pastors there that I called the fifteenth chapter of John "The Pruning Chapter" and as I spoke to that group of men I brought out the illustration of God as the Sovereign Vine Keeper and tiller of the soil. And that God will take out His Divine pruning knife on each person serious with Him. He must cut on us with His Divine knife and prune back, strip away, any excess that hinders His work and our usefulness for the purpose of our increased fruitfulness to bring Him glory!

And midway through my message, while my two intercessors were busy at the back of the room with bowed heads in prayer, I noticed that the countenances of the pastor's was suddenly altered from smiling to looks of concern. God had showed up and was dealing with each of those men. And when it was over a line formed to shake my hand and thank me for the message delivered, and standing before me was an elderly black pastor and he wrapped his arms around me and hugged me tight and with tears in his eyes he said, "I've been a pastor for forty years. But tonight I'm gonna go home and get down by my bed and pray for the Lord to take out His pruning knife on me and my ministry!" That man was ready to get serious with God in revival!

On another occasion I was out of town vacationing in Florida with no intent on doing any ministry work. I just wanted to relax and play some golf. But two weeks earlier a pastor from this part of Florida visited Memphis to attend a Stephen Olford institute for preaching and that is how I met him. He had gotten a copy of my first book on revival, "Realities Of Revival" and he wanted to talk about it. So when I was in his town I located his church and called him up to see what time they had Wednesday evening service because I wished to visit them. He gave me the time for worship and I hung up the phone. Thirty minutes later he called me (this was around 3pm) and he asked me to take the Wednesday evening service and bring a message for them. I said I'd pray about it and hung up the phone. Well, I didn't even have a suit with me as I was on vacation. But I prayed about it and after another thirty minutes I called him back to accept the invitation to preach that evening.

I showed up at the church with no sermon. I walked in with just my bible and looking around at the people there I decided to turn to Amos, chapter four. I announced my text and read it. I related to them that Amos was a country preacher, who had been a sheep breeder, and had been called by God to be His prophet. And that even his name, Amos, meant "burden" and that God had given him a burden for the Jews to return to God in heartfelt repentance. But they refused to heed his warnings and they refused to repent. He had a tough going of it as a preacher whose message merely fell on deaf ears.

I began my message out of Amos chapter four and verse six:

> *"And I also have given you cleanness of teeth in all your cities, and want of bread in all*

your places: yet have ye not returned unto me, saith the LORD."

I told them that God was displeased with the Jews because of their backslidings, and half-hearted worship of Him. That they had fallen into idolatry and sensuality and God began to send them His remedial judgments to get them to return to Him. But they refused to listen. And the judgements became more and more severe. I said that God sent His people a famine in the land, but they refused to turn back to Him. Then I read them verse 7:

"And also I have withholden the rain from you, there were yet three months to the harvest: and I caused it to rain upon one city, and caused it not to rain upon another city: one piece was rained upon, and the piece whereupon it rained not withered."

And I told those people sitting there that this was a remedial judgement that came to them because the first judgment went unheeded and that brough a judgment upon them of increased severity. Because a person can go a week without food, but man cannot live long without water. So God sent them a terrible drought. And how did they respond? "Yet have ye not returned unto me, saith the LORD."

Then I read them verse 9 which declares:

"I have smitten you with blasting and mildew; when your gardens and your vineyards and your fig trees and your olive trees increased, the palmerworm devoured them: yet have ye not returned unto me, saith the LORD."

I told the people that this was a very serious increased remedial judgment from God upon them for it described a financial collapse. Their crops were ruined. And then I told them how shaky the American economy was and that it was a house of cards that any strong wind could blow down quite suddenly in a severe stock market crash. I knew what I was talking about because in my secular job I was a stockbroker. I told them that God sent them a famine, then severe drought, then a economic crash that hit their pocketbooks and bank accounts. But still the stiff-necked Jews would not repent and turn back to God! Then I said, God had to get drastic with them. I read them verse 10 which states: "I have sent among you the pestilence after the manner of Egypt: your young men have I slain with the sword, and have taken away your horses; and I have made the stink of your camps to come up unto your nostrils; yet have ye not returned unto me, saith the LORD."

I told them how God was a God who kills people. And because of their stubbornness and spiritual deadness He had to cut some of them off and kill them with a pestilence and sword. I told them that when you remove the young men from a community there is little hope left for that community---that this was a dreadful judgement from an offended Sovereign God.

I then prayed and closed the meeting and dismissed them. When it was over the people left the sanctuary quickly and quietly. The pastor approached me and commented: "When I preach to them they leave here smiling and laughing and talking. But when you preached to them tonight, their eyes were red and "they left in complete silence." Well that told me something was going on here and God was going to do a work in their midst.

That was a Wednesday. On Thursday, the pastor of the church telephoned me to ask me if I could address the men of the church on Saturday morning around say, 10am. He said that if I came to the church Saturday at 10am he would have a room full of men to hear me. I prayed about it. I soon realized that God didn't want me to relax and play golf on this vacation, but I was to be active in His service because He was getting ready to do something with this church.

On Saturday morning we met at 10am. The room was full of men who looked real serious. I started us in prayer. And then I read to them out of a book I wrote on repentance, called "Return To Me." and I read them 75 things that displeased God.

The men were bowed down on their knees while I spoke and they went to praying and talking to God. They were getting serious with God. Two and a half hours later, we broke for lunch. At 1:30pm we met again in the same room and I spoke on the need for revival and what that entailed. This meeting didn't end until 5pm. We had spent all day Saturday getting serious with God.

Well, I was worn out. and I told the pastor that I was leaving in the morning to head back home to Tennessee for my vacation was over and I had to be at work on Monday morning. Late that Saturday evening I got a phone call from that pastor begging me to stay and take the Sunday morning service. I didn't know what to do. I had to be back to work on Monday—so I called my friend Al Whittinghill, to ask him what he thought I should do. I explained to him what had been transpiring at the church since I'd been preaching. He said to stay. I said I had no sermon prepared for tomorrow morning and I had to be back in Tennessee. Al said it was obvious God was at work and I needed to stay and preach Sunday morning. So I did.

I didn't have a suit or even a white shirt. I showed up to preach wearing a ten year old pair of pants, a beige long sleeve shirt and an old tie I found in the drawer of my condo. I looked in the mirror and to myself I looked like a fool. But I went anyhow and preached my heart out that morning because I had spent most of the night out of bed on my knees in prayer for those people in that church!

When I arrived at the church I met the pastor in his study where we spent some time in prayer. The pastor recognized that God was at work among his people and this pastor was a real man of prayer. The pastor told me he was going to miss my sermon that morning, as he had decided to remain in his study on his knees and on his face before God in prayer during the whole time I was to preach!

I stood before the congregation of about 500 people and I took my text from the Book of Revelation, chapter 20 on the Final Judgment Day. I read them the following striking passage of Scripture:

> *"And I saw a great white throne, and him that sat on it, from whose face the earth and the heaven fled away; and there was found no place for them."*

I told them that this was the great dissolution of all things on earth and the beginning of eternity.

> *"And I saw the dead, small and great, stand before God; and the books were opened: and another book was opened, which is the book of life: and the dead were judged out of those things which were written in the books, according to their works. And the*

sea gave up the dead which were in it; and death and hell delivered up the dead which were in them: and they were judged every man according to their works. And death and hell were cast into the lake of fire. This is the second death. And whosoever was not found written in the book of life was cast into the lake of fire."

Then I closed my bible. And I faced them. I told them about a cardiologist who was an atheist. And this atheist heart surgeon saw some things on the operating table that shocked him and he couldn't explain them. He saw dead people come back to live. Patients who died on the operating table and were clinically dead, suddenly came back to life and spoke of their visit to hell itself! And this scared the cardiologist and he began to read the bible to see what it had to say about life after death. And this atheist doctor studied the bible until he was completely saved and brought to Christ. And he wrote book about it, about these patients of his who had died and visited hell and came back and told what they had seen. And he put all their stories in this book, entitled, *"To Hell and Back"* and it became a bestseller.

And then I went back to my text in Revelation about the last judgment and I told them that every one of them, every mother's son would stand there on that day. And their lives would be reviewed by the one sitting on that Great White throne. I said the white of that throne speaks of God's holiness. That God is holy and man is sinful. And there is a coming day of reckoning where the law of God will be held up against the works of sinners, and the law in all its strictness and severity will reveal the rottenness of man. All our dirty deeds will be brought to light. The books will be opened on our lives on That Day! The One sitting there on that Great White Throne has eyes of fire and He will review our entire life beneath His intense scrutiny! And if we stand there in our own merits, we will fail that test: *"For all have sinned and come short of the glory of God."* I told them that the sentencing of the law will be carried out upon all guilty lawbreakers! And if you stand there in your natural condition in your own rotten and stained merits you will fail that test—you must stand there in the merits of another—The Lord Jesus Christ!

And about two thirds of the way in my sermon I looked out on the congregation and I saw that their faces were altered with great looks of concern. It was as if a cannon ball had been shot down the middle aisle of that church! I gave the invitation to come to Christ for salvation of sin. I asked for the deacons of the church to come down front and counsel those who may need prayer. But nobody came. Nobody stirred. I thought perhaps they failed to understand me. So once more I asked for the deacons to come down front and stand at the platform in case anyone needed prayer and counseling. Nobody came. Nobody stirred. Surprised, I grabbed my bible and sat down on the front row with my back to them. I dropped to my knees with my arms raised over my head as I began to worship a holy God. I had done what I was supposed to do—preach to them. It was now up to Him. I just wanted to worship Him for who He is!

Suddenly, a young man came bounding down the aisle, jumping up and down, and hollering, "I just got saved! I just got saved! I really just got saved!" others began to come forward. After the service the music minister had a big grin on his face and he said, "I saw Jesus. I saw Jesus sitting on His throne!"

One of the deacons approached me to apologize for not coming forward when I asked them to come. He said, "We couldn't come. It was as if we were frozen in our seats and we could not get up!"

I am only relating to you what they said to me. But God was at work that day in that church and that week. That is revival!

CHAPTER SEVEN
MEN OF REVIVAL

"The Apostle Paul, Luther, Wesley, Whitefield, Knox, Edwards, Finney, Spurgeon, Moody, Jones, each shared a common denominator: a fire in their belly. They each were so eaten up with the Gospel and thirsty for Christ and filled with the Holy Ghost—they could not stand idly by while others perished. They saw nothing but eternity, worshipped a Holy God, and served a Risen Christ. Living not for earth nor its gains but living only for heaven and its rewards. When they preached, they linked the Devil with sin and the Cross with salvation. They preached hell and its fire and Christ and Him crucified. Not one of them feared King, Queen, or Pope; and not one of them sought the compliments of men."

E. A. Johnston

It is extremely important that we study the men God has used in revival in former times. It is imperative to study the life of George Whitefield and John Wesley and what God did through them to awaken a nation. We must make it our priority to be deeply familiar with the lives of Jonathan Edwards and David Brainerd, and be familiar with all the secondary figures of the Great Awakening and Second Great Awakening. How will we be able to recognize a true revival if it were to come if we have not spent the time to study how God has moved in former times? A spurious so-called revival will fool many and deceive multitudes. There is much false fire out there in history, that sparks up every now and then but God is not in it. We must carefully read the biographies of men of revival to learn how God uses men in revival! We must know the facts of historic revival and not believe mere fables passed down by those not acquainted with the facts.

George Whitefield was the primary human instrument of the Revival of Religion in England, not John Wesley. Asahel Nettleton was the primary human instrument of the Second Great Awakening, not Charles Finney. But history has a way of taking the leader of a movement and making him secondary and lifting up the second figure and making him primary. But whatever part each man played in the revival they each were holy men of God and mightily used of God.

Jonathan Edwards was unquestionably the main figure of the Great Awakening in the Colonies. The fires of revival began with him in Northhampton, Mass., but at his invitation, George Whitefield came and poured gasoline on it! In 1740, George Whitefield preached to twenty thousand hearers on Boston Common and everywhere Whitefield went a revival started!

We see from the following observations by Martyn Lloyd-Jones:

"He would preach on Moorfields Common, he would preach in Marylebone, Fields— just north of the present Marylebone Road. He would preach in what was then called May Fair, which we now call 'Mayfair'. He used to preach on Kennington Common. He used to preach on Blackheath. Indeed, in any place where there was a great open space Whitefield had but to get up and to preach and thousands crowded to listen to him. His average congregation was somewhere in the neighborhood of twenty thousand people at a time, and, remember, they all had to stand. But they stood willingly.

"He just went on doing this for the rest of his life. He did this all over England, he did it in Wales…in Scotland…in America. Thus this phenomenon continued. When it was heard that he was in the neighborhood and about to preach, shopkeepers shut their shops at once, for they must hear him; businessmen forgot their business, farmers put down their tools.

"He could get a congregation of thousands any time of day or night; he could get them and hold them in snow, sleet, frost, rain—it did not matter what the conditions were. In America in one very cold winter they used to stand by the thousands listening to this man preaching the gospel, and they would travel endless distances in order to get this great opportunity and privilege.[3]

Both John Wesley and George Whitefield suffered great persecution for preaching the gospel. Whitefield would preach while being pelted with rotten eggs and pieces of dead cats; one time he was stoned while preaching in Ireland and almost died. When in America, while preaching in Boston, he was introduced to a minister from Ireland, to which Whitefield removed his beaver cap and learning forward pointed to a large scar on his forehead with the remark: "This Sir, is the wound I received whilst preaching Christ in your country!"

John Wesley faced similar persecution for preaching Christ. His brother Charles wrote in his diary, "Today my brother John was dragged by a mob by his hair through the town.

---

[3] E. A. Johnston, "George Whitefield A Definitive Biography Volumes 1 and 2" (Georgia: Old Paths Publications, 2023). P 175.

And he escaped a large stone hurled at him because of his diminutive size." But God used John Wesley in revival after revival because of his great faith. Wesley cried: "Give me one hundred men who fear nothing but God, and hate nothing but sin, and I will shake the gates of hell." And he did just that!

It was said of Asahel Nettleton by his good friend, Bennet Tyler (Founder of Hartford Seminary) "he was the means of 30,000 souls being brought to Christ." When I was researching my definitive biography on Nettleton's life and ministry I visited over sixty locations throughout four States in which Asahel Nettleton saw mighty revivals! Here is his own account of one such revival in Schenectady, NY taken from his diary in his personal papers at Hartford Seminary: "The revival is now very powerful in the city. Such a scene they never before witnessed. More than one hundred have been brought to rejoice in hope. Besides these, we had more than two hundred in our meetings of inquiry, anxious for their souls. We met in a large upper room called The Masonic Hall. The room was so crowded, that we were obliged to request all who had recently found relief, to retire below, and spend their time in prayer for those above. This evening will never be forgotten. The scene is beyond description. Did you ever witness two hundred sinners, with one accord in one place, weeping for their sins. Until you have seen this, you can have no adequate conceptions of the solemn scene. I felt as though I was standing on the verge of the eternal world; while the floor under my feet was shaken by the trembling of anxious souls in view of a judgment to come. This solemnity was still heightened, when every knee was bent at the throne of grace, and the intervening silence of the voice of prayer, was interrupted only by the sighs and sobs of anxious souls. I have not time to relate interesting particulars, I only add, that some of the most stout, hard-hearted, heaven-daring rebels have been in the most awful distress. Within a circle whose diameter would be twenty four miles, not less than eight hundred souls have been hopefully born into the kingdom of Christ, since last September. The same glorious work is fast spreading into other towns and congregations.

'This is what was spoken by the prophet Joel.'"[4]

---

4 E. A. Johnston, "Asahel Nettleton Biography: Revival Preacher" (Georgia: Old Paths Publications, 2023). P 148.

Another evangelist mightily used in revival is a man many are not familiar with, Rolfe Barnard canvassed America in the late 1920's to 1960's as a evangelist who saw incredible revivals where entire towns were affected by the power of God. The following accounts are indicative of his mighty ministry. Often those who fought against a revival would face God's swift hammer of justice as seen in the following account taken from Rolfe Barnard's sermon, "Sudden Death":

The pastor of a church in a certain place asked me to come and hold meetings. Before I got there, seven deacons of that church had come to the pastor and said, "Now Brother Pastor, we are not going to oppose anything, but we don't believe in what you call evangelistic campaigns. So we will not be back until this preacher is gone and the meetings are over." The pastor said, "Well, I hate to see you take that attitude, but if that is what you want to do, I appreciate you coming and telling me."

Well, if they had done what they said, it would have been all right. But we couldn't get a crowd for a few nights and we were hitting it pretty hard. So those fellows were glad and got to bragging about how we weren't getting anywhere in the meetings. They violated their word that they wouldn't oppose us.

The pastor came to me and he was brokenhearted he said, "Brother Barnard, this is killing me, what can we do?'" I said, "I don't know. Are you game for us to get down on our knees and ask God to save them or kill them? He agreed, and we got down on our knees and said, "Lord, You know what these fellows are doing. They are ruining the meeting, they are making fun of the gospel, the church, and the Lord Jesus Christ and God's preachers." They were just filling the whole town with this, and everybody was talking about how the meeting was no good, and those seven deacons making fun of it. And so we said, "Lord, save them or kill them!"

Neither one of us was supposed to tell about that prayer and I don't think I did, but somebody did, and those deacons heard about it. They just heard half of it, though, and so they just had a big time. They said, "The preachers up there are praying for God to kill us!" But we were praying for God to save them or kill them, to get them out of the way. They were bucking God, they were hardening themselves against God. I think that is dangerous. They just laughed and had a big time about it. But in four days time, the pastor had seven different funerals, and they were the funerals of those seven Baptist deacons. Every one of them died a horrible sudden death! God kills people that harden themselves against His claims for Jesus Christ![5]

The next story demonstrates God's grace in salvation under Barnard's searching preaching. This event took place in the State of Texas in 1928 when Rolfe Barnard was a seminary student. The story is taken from Rolfe Barnard's sermon entitled, "God's Call":

In Texas many years ago while I was a student in Southwestern Seminary there was a little mining town nearby. And I went one summer while I was in school and held what is called revival services. I began the meeting there on Sunday night. I got up that night and I preached; I remember I preached on hell that night and dismissed the congregation, praying that the Holy Spirit would speak to hearts and disturb people.

As we stood there something touched my shoulder. I looked around and the old white-

---

[5] E. A. Johnston, "God's Hitchhike Evangelist, The Biography Of Rolfe Barnard", (Georgia: Old Paths Publications, 2023). P 62.

haired pastor stood there, his face drenched in tears. He said, "Brother Preacher might I say a few words?" Of course, he might, and he said, "Folks, let's don't go home for a few minutes. I just can't let you go right now." Somebody happened to look at his watch and exactly thirty-three minutes later a lot had happened. That pastor stood there with his face in tears, and he pointed men out and called them by their given name. I had never seen anything like it! He had been pastor there over thirty years. He knew them by their given name. He said, "Bill, I just can't let you go tonight," and he preached to Bill, and here came Bill. "Jim," and he did that to thirty-three men, one by one. Nobody left. He just called those men by name and talked to them, and here they came.

Thirty-three minutes later thirty-three men were lined up! I don't know whether they got saved or not—I'll find out at the judgment. I simply know this—they claimed to. There was power there that night. There was Somebody there beside us. God used that preacher to talk to those men through him. He couldn't use me, but He used him. We had an old-fashioned hand shaking! We had thirty-three men professing their faith in Christ!

Everybody made their living in the coal mine. But Monday night I didn't preach. I was going to preach, but they didn't have service Monday night. At 4:26 p.m., Monday, one of the mines had an explosion and caved in, and some men were buried in that mine. And the whistle blew and sirens and alarms went off in that little mining town, and all they did was to gather at that mine with all their equipment. And while they worked feverishly, some prayed, some cried, and some cursed!

But they worked to get down to where those men were trapped. The time keeper or whoever is in charge of time consulted his books and knew there were thirty-three men trapped down in that mine. They worked feverishly and finally they got to them, and one by one, they hauled up the bodies of those thirty-three men who were crushed in that mine. Every one of them were dead, and they were the thirty-three men that lined up there and said they had received Christ![6]

---

[6] Ibid. pp 63-64.

CHAPTER EIGHT
THE MAN GOD USES

"God's eyes are continually searching the earth for those rare individuals of 'whom the world was not worthy.' Men like Moses and John the Baptist; Luther and Calvin; Whitefield and Wesley; Finney and Moody. Men who live in a different atmosphere than other mortals; men who have annihilated self with the Cross and whose lives are broken alabaster boxes from which fragrances arise to the heavens from the broken pieces of selflessness, self-sacrifice, and self-crucifixion. God is always on the 'look out' for such men."

E. A. Johnston

When one studies the history of revival and reads biographies on men that God has used in seasons of revival, it is truly remarkable that God seems pleased to use men not for their learning and education, not for their talents and winning personality, but because they were simple men who were entirely surrendered to God. God took a uneducated, rough man who could not even properly spell the word "bed" and used him to shake Great Britain in revival for God (D. L. Moody). God took a broken-down alcoholic lawyer and used him to transform the moral and spiritual life of entire cities in powerful revivals (Sam Jones). God took a youth of divorced parents who was raised in a tavern with a physical deformity of a noticeable squint in his eye and used him to shake two continents for God in powerful revival and spiritual awakening (George Whitefield). God took a broken-down pastor in his fifties and placed him in the midst of a four-year long revival, 1949-1952 on the Isle of Lewis in the Hebrides of Scotland to where it was said the entire island was saturated with the presence of God (Duncan Campbell). God took an asthmatic, sickly old man of 53, who against all doctors' orders and against the pleas of his wife and family, to take a one way trip into the heart of Africa to preach the gospel of the Son of God to the heathens, and sparked fires of revival in missionary enterprise (C. T. Studd). God took the President of the Atheist Club on a college campus to canvas America in a evangelistic preaching ministry that would transform entire towns in revival after revival (Rolfe Barnard). God took a man out of China sent him to America to be educated and then placed him against his will in an insane asylum for 193 days and then sent him back to China to shake China for God in ground shaking miracle working revival after revival! (John Sung). God took an obstinate lawyer with no theological training and thrust him into a itinerant ministry in Western New York during the Second Great Awakening and used him in powerful revivals that had his hearers fall out of their chairs, crying out to God, quicker than if he had a sword in two hands he could not have cut them down fast enough (Charles Finney).

God took a man….and used him for His glory (this could be your story). I once asked a minister on the isle of Lewis who knew Duncan Campbell personally to describe to me in one sentence Duncan Campbell. He said, "Duncan Campbell was an ordinary man who had had an extraordinary experience of God." I believe the same can be said of Moses, David, Abraham, Jacob, Joseph. God took a murderer and a fugitive who became a lowly sheep herder on the backside of the desert to work miracles and deliver a nation (Moses). God took a shepherd boy and made him a king (David). God took a ordinary man in whom he built faith and made him the father of a nation (Abraham). God took a man so crooked he could hide behind a corkscrew and used him time and time again to bring Him glory (Jacob). God took a youth whose brothers turned against him and was sold into slavery to lead an entire nation (Joseph).

The man God uses is a man willing to go out on a limb for Him and risk his reputation and his skin to do something great for God and eternity! What costs counts and what counts costs. The man God uses is a man willing to take risks for God and to risk his very life if necessary for Christ and the Gospel! God is looking for the Peter's who are willing to step out of the boat on faith and walk on the water with Him! The man God uses is a man who once he gets a taste of the supernatural no longer desires the safety of the boat! The man God uses is a man of prayer. A man empty of self and ambition. A man full of the Holy Ghost. A man entirely surrendered to the Lordship of Jesus Christ! The man God uses is a man willing to face fierce persecution for Christ and the souls of men!

Mordecai Ham was a man of God used mighty in revivals all over 20th century America.

He faced hot persecution in every city he preached in and in every city he preached in he saw powerful revivals that transformed the moral life of the community. Mordecai Ham set up a tent in the red light district of a town and preached every day for four weeks straight until the brothels had to close their doors and go out of business because all the girls had been saved. Mordecai Ham was pistol whipped, captured by a gang of men and dragged out of town to be tarred, feathered and hung from a tree—he was only rescued when the mayor of the city called in the calvary to save him. Mordecai Ham was run over by a car, hired by the liquor trade, and he spent the next six months in the hospital in a coma. Upon leaving his hotel one evening, he was attacked in the hotel lobby from behind by a man with a quirk. But, besides all this, Mordecai Ham was preaching one night when a teenage church member in good standing came to hear him and became mad at the preacher for pointing him out as a big sinner. That young man was brought to Christ that night and saved (Billy Graham).[7]

---

[7] Edward E. Ham, "50 Years On The Battlefront with Christ, A Biography Of Mordecai Ham. (Nashville; The Old Kentucky Home Revivalist: 1950) pp 77-219.

The man God uses is a man who wants to be used of God more than he wants to use his life for his own pleasure, comforts, and gain.

CHAPTER NINE
JONATHAN EDWARDS

"Jonathan Edwards knew the cost of revival. After seeing God move in several seasons of glorious revival, the last fourteen years of Edward's life were filled with trouble, trial, grief, opposition, turmoil, and termination. He had to witness the early death of his young friend, David Brainerd. Four months later he suffered the personal loss of the sudden death of his eighteen-year-old daughter, Jerusha. He was then thrust into a scene of great controversy and opposition in his own church which resulted in his removal. He and his large family were suddenly thrust into privation and cast upon the world with no financial support and he ended up in the wilderness of Stockbridge, MA with a ministry of preaching to a mere handful of

Indians. While laboring there in inclement weather he came down with a severe fever that made him an invalid for a period of seven months, which greatly weakened his already strained constitution. From there he had a brief promotion to President of the College of New Jersey, only to die before assuming his labors at the age of 54 from a fatal reaction to a new vaccine. He died with the weight of the world upon him as he entered a better world, where pain, suffering, and struggle were no more.

By the way, did I mention that these last fourteen years of his life was his greatest period of productivity, whereby he wrote the bulk of his written legacy to the Church at large."

E. A. Johnston

The man that God uses continued…. Jonathan Edwards was a tall thin sickly man who was endowed with one of the greatest minds in the history of the church. He was a man completely surrendered to God and greatly useful to God. He was more deeply familiar the time period known as The Great Awakening, than most of the men who lived through it. He has written more wisely on the subject of revival than any man living since or before him.

Most of the world is only familiar with him as an outdated, puritanical preacher from New England who was known for one sermon, entitled, "Sinners In The Hands Of An Angry God." But he deserves to be studied. Deserves to be read. Jonathan Edwards preached searching sermons which brought his hearers to the very verge of eternity. I have walked the ground in Enfield, Connecticut, which is now a field with a stone marker commemorating the spot where Edwards preached that famous sermon in a meeting house on July 8th, 1741. An eyewitness account relates the following: "We went over to Enfield—where we met dear Mr. E of NH who preached a most awakening sermon from these words—Deut. 32-35 and before sermon was done—there was a great moaning and crying out through ye Whole House—What Shall I do to be saved—oh I am going to Hell—

Oh what shall I do for Christ &c. So ye minister was obliged to desist—ye shrieks and cries were piercing and Amazing--."[8]

I would highly recommend the reading of Edward's sermon, "Sinners In The Hands Of An Angry God" as mandatory reading for any serious student of revival!

Also every student of revival needs to study his magnum opus on revival: "A Faithful Narrative of the surprising work of God in the conversion of many hundred souls in Northampton, and the neighboring towns and villages of New Hampshire in New England."

We must be deeply familiar with how God moved in former times in revival and spiritual awakening in the land, if we are to be able to recognize a true revival of religion if it were to take place in our time. Also, studying about historical revivals will teach us how to better pray for revival in our time. Also, there is a vast difference about preaching about revival and preaching for revival. Preaching about revival is relating to others revival stories and accounts of historical revival. Whereas

---

[8] Oliver Means, "A Sketch of the Strict Congregational Church of Enfield, Conn." (Hartford: 1899). P 192.

preaching for revival is to preach doctrinally with the purpose of awakening a sleeping church to recognize her need for revival!

CHAPTER TEN
VISITING SCENES OF REVIVAL

"To stand where Whitefield stood, Wesley stood, Edwards stood, Finney stood, Moody and Jones stood, and to allow one's mind to replay the very scene that transpired there two hundred years ago, is both invigorating for personal witness and igniting to spiritual living. Tracing the steps of men whom God has used in former times of revival is a unforgettable experience that will last a lifetime."

E. A. Johnston

I have had the privilege of visiting many scenes of revival throughout America and Great Britain. I have carefully retraced the steps of men like George Whitefield, John Wesley, Jonathan Edwards, Asahel Nettleton, D. L. Moody, Sam Jones. When I was conducting my research on the life and ministry of Asahel Nettleton, the primary leader of the Second Great Awakening, I personally visited over sixty locations in four States where he preached and saw powerful revivals. When I was conducting my research on my definitive biography of the great British evangelist, George Whitefield, I traveled extensively through America from Savannah, Ga up to Charleston, SC throughout New England and Maine. In Great Britain I retraced Whitefield's steps in England, Scotland, and Wales.

In this chapter we will provide revival locations for you to travel to and research on your own. This is not a comprehensive list of revival locations but a overview of some of the more well known locations where God had been pleased to move in former times with His choice servants. We hope this part of the book is of some practical worth as to visiting actual scenes of revival that you can conduct on your own time.

JONATHAN EDWARDS

The town of Northampton, MA is of primary importance to students of Jonathan Edwards. The location of his church, home, and labors can be visited in a single day trip. A visit to Bridgestreet Cemetery is also suggested (where are the graves of Solomon Stoddard, David Brainerd, Jerusha Edwards).

The town of East Windsor, CT has the birthplace of Jonathan Edwards (marked by a plaque) as well as the cemetery where his father Timothy Edwards is buried.

In Enfield, CT is a large commemorative stone marker denoting the place of the old meeting house in which Edwards preached his famous sermon in July of 1741, *"Sinners In The Hands Of An Angry God."*

GEORGE WHITEFIELD

There are Whitefield locations all over New England, but the primary ones can be found in the following locations: Newburyport, MA, The Old South Presbyterian Church, where Whitefield's remains are buried in the crypt of the church beneath the pulpit. He lies beneath a slab between Jonathan Parsons, the first pastor of the church, and a blind Indian preacher who labored with Whitefield.

The house where Whitefield died is three houses from the church and is a personal residence today. Whitefield died in the upper bedroom window on the left side of the house.

Exeter, NH in the town square is a large stone with the word Whitefield engraved upon it marking the spot of his last sermon which he preached for two hours in the open air in the fields of Exeter. This is the location of the famous Whitefieldian quote:

"I'd rather wear out than rust out."

As he slowly and laboriously approached the preaching place a man said to him: "Mister Whitefield, you look more fit for bed than to preach." To which the grand itinerant replied, "Quite true Sir. But I'd rather wear out than rust out!"

There is a rock in Ipswich, MA called "Pulpit Rock" whereupon Whitefield preached on several occasions.

In Charleston, SC is an existing church which Whitefield preached in. Saint Michael's Church at 71 Broad Street. The original pulpit is still in use. Also over at Saint Phillip's Church is the graveyard where Whitefield's fiercest opponent lies buried, Alexander Garden, who tried to get Whitefield excommunicated from the Anglican Church!

In Savannah, GA is the orphan home Whitefield founded: Bethesda Home For Boys (it is the oldest operating orphanage in the United States). Hanging there is a full-length portrait of Selina, Countess of Huntington, Whitefield's main supporter from England. He was her chaplain and it was she who introduced Whitefield to the royalty of Great Britain so he could preach Christ to them.

Great Britain is George Whitefield country! England, Scotland, Ireland, and Wales have Whitefield locations galore. The list is too long to mention here (see my definitive 1,200 page biography on Whitefield, two volumes in one, paperback).

JOHN WESLEY

In London, England is the grave of John Wesley, as well as his church (both across from Bunhill Fields) and museum housing his memorabilia including his pulpit from Moorfields, his collar, gown, etc.

In London there is a plaque commemorating the place of John Wesley's conversion at Aldersgate Street.

In Bristol, England is the church and home of Wesley which can be visited with a led tour guide.

All over England are John Wesley sites and locations where he preached in great revivals.

In Savannah, Georgia, John Wesley labored unsuccessfully as a missionary before he was truly born again.

D. L. MOODY

One cannot thoroughly study Moody without visiting Northfield, MA, his birthplace and center of operations for much of his life. Still standing is the home he was born in. and down the hill the home he died in.

Moody's grave is on Round Top, site of his many sermons during his Northfield Conferences.

The old Auditorium still stands, where countless famous preachers spoke: men like G. Campbell Morgan, F. B. Myer, C. T. Studd, Scofield, Torrey, and Sam Jones.

There is a museum in the house Moody was born in and it is a treasure trove of Moody's life: his death mask, his writing desk, his bible, Sankey's organ, and other memorabilia is housed there.

Moody's famous portrait by Healey hangs on the wall of the home he was born in. This is the portrait Moody had under his arm as he and his family fled the great Chicago Fire. He only took it at his wife's insistence, remarking to her as they left the house, "What is that you are clinging to so dearly Moody? Is that your likeness!"

SAM JONES

In Cartersville, GA is the home of Sam Jones. Today it is a museum called: Rose Lawn and is open for tours.

The grave of Sam Jones is also in Cartersville.

Boston, MA is the location of Faneuil Hall where Sam Jones preached to four thousand men in a remarkable revival.

Nashville, TN, Ryman Auditorium was built by Capt. Thomas Ryman, a convert of Sam Jones, for Sam Jones to preach in

Any major city in America: Atlanta, Memphis, Nashville, St. Louis, Kansas City, Chicago, Baltimore, Boston, and New York City have churches and locations where Sam Jones preached and saw incredible revivals. Also, any town or city in the State of Georgia is Sam Jones' country! (see my biography on Sam Jones).

ASAHEL NETTLETON

Hartford Seminary was founded by Asahel Nettleton and houses his personal papers, as well as two hand written letters by Jonathan Edwards.

East Windsor, CT is where the grave of Asahel Nettleton is and the home in which he died.

There are many locations throughout New England that are historical scenes of revival where Nettleton was mightily used of God in the Second Great Awakening (see my definitive biography on Nettleton).

CHAPTER ELEVEN
PREPARING FOR REVIVAL

"God used Finney as a human instrument of revival in the early stages of the Second Great Awakening. Where Finney erred is when he relegated revival from a sovereign act of God to a mere methodology whereby man could "create revival" anytime he wanted to so long as it was a thing desired and acted upon."

E. A. Johnston

One of the best studies for any student of revival is the Cambuslang Revival in Scotland of 1742. It is a textbook pattern for the church to prepare for revival using the proper means. Although man cannot produce revival on his own as it is a sovereign work of God, the people of God can prepare their hearts and properly align themselves to God in the expectation that God will send His revival wind.

There was a country pastor in Cambuslang, Scotland outside of Glasgow, by the name of William M'Culloch. What he lacked in ability as a preacher he made up for in his tremendous faith to see revival come to his church. He was such a poor speaker and dry as dust that he was called "ye ale minster"; for when he got up to preach it was said the people left to go to the ale house for a drink. He became deeply interested in the revival in the Colonies under Jonathan Edwards in Northampton, MA and voraciously read any printed material he could obtain from America relating the revival. He began to read his congregation accounts of these revivals with the hopes of stirring an interest in them for revival. Once his people were thirsty for revival then he altered his preaching to doctrinal preaching where he preached an entire series of sermons on regeneration and the utter necessity of being born again. This was attended by the Holy Spirit in conviction and soon the people were in quite a commotion deeply concerned about their eternal welfare. Then William M'Culloch invited George Whitefield to come visit his parish and preach to his people and when that happened a powerful revival took over the church and region and it was so remarkable in its intensity and fruitfulness it even startled Whitefield himself who wrote in a letter to his wife the following account:

"At noon I came to Cambuslang, the place which GOD hath so much honored. I preached at two, to a vast body of people, and at six in the evening, and again at nine at night. Such a commotion surely was never was heard of, especially at eleven at night. If far out-did all that I ever saw in America. For about an hour and a half there was such weeping, so many falling into deep distress, and expressing it various ways, as is inexpressible. The people seem to be slain by scores. They are carried off, and come into the house like soldiers wounded in, and carried off a field of battle. Their cries and agonies are exceedingly affecting. Mr. M'Culloch preached after I ended, till past one in the morning, and then could scarce persuade them to depart. All night in the fields, might be heard the voice of prayer and praise. Some young ladies were found by a gentlewoman praising GOD at break of day. The LORD indeed is much with me. I have preached twice today already, and am to preach twice, perhaps three times more. The commotions increase. [9]

Notice several elements of what took place before George Whitefield arrived—first, the revival was already commenced. There was an awakening in M'Culloch's people which was the result of his reading them revival accounts by Jonathan Edwards from the revival in Northampton, MA., and the change to doctrinal preaching on regeneration and man's need of it for salvation. God honored this preparatory work and heaven sent revival ensued with great power! This pattern can be replicated by any pastor of any church. First, there has to be an interest in revival; then there has to be an acknowledgment of the need for

---

[9] E. A. Johnston, "George Whitefield A Definitive Biography, Two Volumes In One", (Georgia: Old Paths Publications, 2023), Volume Two, pp 595-596.

revival; then there has to be doctrinal preaching with searching sermons which probe the conscience of the hearers. Since salvation is in the hands of God and not man, only God can open hearts---but it is up to us to prepare our hearts so the blessings of grace can fall!

The Revival at Cambuslang was deepening in its power and influence, it is important for us to study this revival so as to be familiar with how the Almighty moves in times of revival. Also, it is imperative that we pay attention to the sermons preached during a revival and the effects of it upon the hearers, as reported by eye witnesses. Below M'Culloch's church was a ravine and a natural amphitheater which became the place of the greatest part of the revival—as the church could not contain the people they moved outdoors to what became known as "the preaching braes." We see from the following eyewitness account:

> "The sacrament at Cambuslang was an event never to be forgotten. Thirteen ministers were present on Friday, Saturday, and Sunday; and, on Monday, twenty-four. All of them

appeared to be very much assisted in their work. Four of them preached on the fast day; four on Saturday, on the Sabbath I cannot tell how many, and five on Monday. Mr. Whitefield's sermons, on Saturday and the two following days, were attended with much power, particularly on Sunday night, and on Monday; several crying out, and a great weeping being observable throughout his auditories. While he was serving some of the tables, he appeared to be so filled with the love of God, as to be in a kind of ecstasy, and he communicated with much of that blessed frame. The numbers present, on the LORD's day were so great, that, so far as I can hear, none ever saw the like since the revolution, in Scotland, or even anywhere else, at any sacrament occasion. This vast concourse of people came, not only from the city of Glasgow, but, from many places at a considerable distance. It was reckoned, that, there were two-hundred communicants from Edinburgh, two-hundred from Kilmarnock, a hundred from Irvine, and a hundred from Stewarton. Some, also, were from England and Ireland. A considerable number of Quakers were hearers. The tables were all served in the open air, beside the tent below the brae. Some estimated the number of persons present at fifty thousand; some at forty thousand; and the lowest estimates were upward of thirty thousand. Not a few were awakened to a sense of sin; others had their bands loosed, and were brought into the liberty of the sons of God; and many of God's children were filled with joy and peace in believing."[10]

---

[10] Ibid. p 605.

The next account of the revival is penned by a hearer who came to hear Whitefield out of curiosity and got saved! It is important to research the actual records of true revivals of religion to see how God deals with the souls of men during times of refreshing! Any worthy study of historical revivals will include eyewitness accounts of remarkable conversions. Here now is one such account:

"Some time in the month of June, 1742, I went to Cambuslang, to hear Mr. Whitefield preach. It was on a Thursday, and his text was, 'The harvest is past, the summer is ended, and we are not saved.' Among other things, he said, 'Many come out of curiosity to hear a poor child preach; and the same curiosity would induce them to go to the devil.' I thought myself described. I had come from no better motive; and I felt that without repentance I could not be saved. Again, addressing God, he said, 'O Lord, how many trample thy blood under their feet, and despise thee and thy gospel!' This led me to such a view of my sins, that I saw nothing but the wrath of God awaiting me, and hell ready to receive me. I was also deeply pierced with a sense of the evil of those sins which I could remember, as well as of the corruption and depravity of my nature and of my unbelief in not receiving but in rejecting Christ, when offered to me in the gospel. My sense of guilt was such, that I would have thought it no injustice, on God's part, had he cast me immediately into hell. I even felt as if I were sinking into the bottomless pit, and that all around were ready to drag me down to it. My feelings of repentance were deep and sincere, and above all, on account of the dishonor which I had done to God.

"Under these awful feelings, I at last fainted away; and on recovering, I was enabled to return with a comrade to my father's house. I attempted to pray, but I could not; my heart was hard as a stone. I had no peace at home, and therefore I returned to Cambuslang, and was in time to hear Mr. M'Culloch's first sermon that day. His text was, 'He hath filled the hungry with good things, and the rich he hath sent empty away' (Luke 1:53). When these words were first read, they came home to my mind with power. I thought much upon them; so much as to lose a considerable part of the sermon. My convictions of sin were so strong, that I was at last forced to cry, nevertheless that I did all I could to restrain myself. I continued in this state during all the time of that sermon, during the interval, and also during the second sermon.

"When it was over, I went alone to pray, pleading with God for grace to close with him

on his own terms; and while so engaged, that saying of Scripture was powerfully borne in upon my mind. *'Fear thou not, for I am with thee: be not dismayed; for I am thy God: I will strengthen thee; yea, I will help thee; yea, I will uphold thee with the right hand of my righteousness,'* (Isaiah 41:10). I was now filled with joy and wonder at what God had done; and thus I was enabled, with all my heart, to believe on Christ—to receive and embrace him so offered in the gospel."[11]

---

[11] Ibid. Volume Two, p 601.

CHAPTER TWELVE
PREACHING FOR REVIVAL

"Anyone who begins to preach for revival will soon face fierce opposition from lost church members. For when the great doctrines of Ruin, Redemption, Repentance, and Regeneration are faithfully proclaimed all hell will break loose."

E. A. Johnston

The Scottish minister, William M'Culloch was a dry unimpressive preacher before his heart was stirred with revival and he changed his message. When he began to preach a series on the doctrine of regeneration to his people and press upon them the utter necessity for a changed heart, then his hearers came under conviction for sin and began to see their lost condition and hell waiting for them.

George Whitefield had one message throughout the Great Awakening, "Ye Must Be Born Again!" While preaching in America on Boston Common to twenty thousand hearers, a minister approached him after service and asked: "Mister Whitefield, since you have been among us all you preach is one message. When Sir will you preach a different message?" To which the great British evangelist replied, "When ye are born again!"

As the message of the Great Awakening was the doctrine of regeneration, the message of the Second Great Awakening was the doctrine of repentance. This was the message of Asahel Nettleton and Charles Finney. Different epochs in history require different emphasis on certain doctrines. Whitefield and Wesley lived in a day of an unconverted ministry, where most of the Episcopal Church of England ministers were unregenerate men. Thus, the message fit the times.

The Second Great Awakening was a day steeped in antinomianism in the church and universalism in society, and the doctrine of repentance was needed to bring the church back to a New Testament standard of holy living.

In our day where the church has shrunken God down to man's size and think of him on a human level then the great need and emphasis would be series of messages on all four doctrines of ruin and redemption, and repentance and regeneration. Man must see his corrupt nature with a bent toward sin to feel his need of a Savior from sin! A sinner must know that his only hope of heaven is be born from above (redemption and regeneration) and washed in the blood (repentance and justification).

There is a vast difference from preaching about the need for revival and actually preaching for revival with doctrinal searching sermons aimed at the conscience of men.

The sad fact is that when the church needs revival the most (in spiritual declension) is when she is least interested in it. Faithful preachers must preach doctrinally sound sermons and preach that sin is black and hell is hot and there is a future judgment that awaits all mankind!

CHAPTER THIRTEEN
FALSE FIRE

"We must be careful when labeling heightened religious activity as revival. Just because there is a sense of the supernatural in worship, religious emotional experience, and growing attendance, does not necessarily denominate a true revival of religion. False fire is the work of Satan from a false spirit that misleads multitudes who ignorant of how God has moved in former times in real periods of revival and awakening. There is a lot of nonsense that has been called 'revival' when God had nothing at all to do with it."

E. A. Johnston

One only has to study the Great Awakening and the sad case of James Davenport, a Congregational minister and itinerant preacher who was noted for his controversial behavior at the height of the revival. After meeting Gilbert Tennent and George Whitefield during the height of the revival, he opened his bible by chance to 1 Samuel 14, where Jonathan and his armor-bearer attack the Philistine camp; and Davenport took this as a sign from God for him to leave his congregation and become a revival preacher. Unfortunately, this overly-excited, emotional man left a trail of great damage to the church of God during the Great Awakening. The culmination of his bizarre behavior happened on March 7, 1743 when he led a large crowd to a bonfire whereby he asked them throw their expensive and fancy clothing into the fire, leading the example he took off his pants and threw them in the fire. One woman immediately pulled his pants out of the fire and handed them back to Davenport pleading with him to regain his senses. He had a habit of denouncing all opposing ministers as unconverted clergymen. After being rebuked publicly by a written notice signed by stellar ministers of the churches in the area, he published a public apology but it was too late to undo all the damage he had done.

Just because there is emotional religious activity is does not characterize a true revival of religion. Satan can do a counter work to revival with a false spirit. Years ago there was a religious movement labeled a revival—called The Toronto Blessing conducted under the auspices of the Toronto Airport Vineyard Church where great crowds assembled to be a part of this "incredible blessing from God". A good friend of mine who was a member of the Vineyard church went and attended the Toronto Blessing. What he related to me afterwards was truly shocking! He said a man behind a microphone would roar like a lion and then the crowd in unison would roar. Then he would lead them in holy laughter until the entire crowd was literally rolling on the ground with hilarious laughter. Bizarre behavior under a religious banner does not make a true revival of religion.

I attended a church where the lead worship singer told a crowd of three thousand people, "The Holy Spirit is here! Can't you feel the Spirit!" and everyone was clapping and swaying to the music and I must admit there was a sense of a "spirit" there but it was not the Holy Spirit—but another.

It is critically important to study historical revivals and become familiar with how God has moved in former times among His people in periods of spiritual awakening and revival. This way knowledge can hold better judgement as to what is the true and the false.

CHAPTER FOURTEEN
THE INSINCERITY OF REVIVAL

"There is a great deal of insincerity concerning revival among the people of God. Many will quote, Second Chronicles 7:14 which states: *"If my people, which are called by my name, shall humble themselves, and pray, and seek my face, and turn from their wicked ways; then will I hear from heaven, and will forgive their sin, and will heal their land."* Very few indeed are willing to comply with all the demands of God in this verse. Many are willing to humble themselves and seek God in prayer for revival, but Hell will freeze over before they ever part with their darling sins and turn from their wicked ways. They are like the man who sincerely desires a deeper walk with God and who is willing to engage in agonizing secret prayer at their own personal Gethsemane—but it stops there.

They fail to go on to Calvary where a Cross awaits, ready to be embraced in a painful, self-exposed crucifixion."

E. A. Johnston

Anything worthwhile in life has a sacrifice attending it. Whether it is higher education or learning a trade. What costs counts and what counts costs. This is true with the desire to see revival in our day.

Dr. Colin N. Peckham wrote the Foreword to one of my books on revival and I will quote him here, as his remarks truly embrace what all revival and praying for revival entails on the part of the people of God:

"Burdened, broken, bold praying is the nerve center of revival. There is a price to be paid, a price of curbed freedom, of resolute concentration, of agonizing supplication. Intercession costs. There is a burden, a passion, an agony, and yes—glory! The breaking through of God into a meeting, the evidence of His felt presence is everything!

"And to get that, costs everything. True intercession is sacrifice. Because of the high demands of taking up this burden, many cannot pay the price and consequently do not gain the rewards and benefits of brokenness and soul-travail in God's presence. Their ministry becomes ordinary; good and biblical, but ordinary! The price is too high. Yet God says, "I the LORD build the ruined places, and plant that that was desolate…I will yet for this be enquired of by the house of Israel, to do it for them" (Ezekiel 36:36-37). Jesus said, "Watch and pray" (Mark 13:33). When last did we pray with broken hearts? When last did we feel that pain-filled fellowship of the pierced hand?"[12]

---

[12] Colin Peckham Foreword to "Sermons For Revival" by E. A. Johnston, (Georgia: Old Paths Publications, 2023) pp 9-10.

CHAPTER FIFTEEN
A NEEDED ENCOUNTER

"When Jesus was here in His earthly ministry, as He passed through towns and villages, those who encountered Him experienced change. Revival is an encounter with Jesus Christ. The Apostle John encountered the Risen Christ on the Isle of Patmos and he fell down as one dead. Revival is a vital encounter with Jesus to where you are dead to sin; dead to self; dead to reputation; and dead to the world. The first concern of those in the midst of revival is the glory of God. The second concern is the salvation of souls. The third concern is a pursuit of holiness unto God."

E. A. Johnston

The Church is a languishing institution beleaguered by a militant pagan society. Through compromise and conformity, she has lost her influence and voice of authority to the nation. As most pulpits are mere teaching platforms there is very little preaching taking place to promote revival.

Apart from the Welsh Revival of 1904 and the Lewis Revival of 1948-1952, one has to go back to the Ulster Revival of 1859 or the Businessman's Prayer Revival of 1858 to have any record of a true revival of religion.

Serious believers, hunger and yearn for a national spiritual awakening which will turn their nation back to the God of the Bible. At the very least, earnest Christians pray regularly for revival to visit their church and community. There is hope in their hearts for a God consciousness in their assemblies once again!

When a people of God are desensitized to sin by the sinful society in which they live; when the people of God lay in spiritual apathy toward the spread of the gospel, and when the people of God have indifference to the lost around them who are perishing and hell-bound—then it is time for AN ENCOUNTER WITH JESUS! We desperately need revival in our day.

CHAPTER SIXTEEN
THE REDUCING OF REVIVAL

"Revival is not only possible, it is probable, as long as we are expendable. God builds His servants through His Divine process of reducing and refining. Gold must be submerged in a refiner's fire of affliction to remove the impurities; a branch must be pruned and decreased before it can grow more fruit. If we desire further usefulness to God then we must submit both to the Refiner's Fire and the Divine Pruning Knife. We must be willing to be reduced to nothing so He can be everything in us."

E. A. Johnston

I was standing in line at seminary for my graduation ceremony to receive my Ph.D., when I asked the pastor standing in line next to me the following question: "How often do you meet with the pastors in your community to pray for revival on a regular basis?"

He looked at me strangely, and replied, "We don't need revival. My church is on the grow." This uniformed pastor mistakes church numerical growth for revival. That to him, a revival is nothing more than more church members and a growing campus of brick and mortar. Unfortunately, many men in ministry believe that their success in ministry is tied to the size of their congregation and number of buildings on their church campus. He who runs three thousand on Sunday is a real success in the minds of many within our denominations.

But the reality is that our religious denominations have fallen into great apostacy and the average pastor does not have a clue about the history of revival—let alone see the need for one to visit his own spiritually dead church.

So we gather each Sunday to sing some songs, shake some hands, and listen to some light teaching from the Bible, interspersed with some funny stories. And this has become the "status quo" for many—"status quo" meaning business as usual. Where are the transformed lives? Where is the power of God in a meeting? Where are the desperate nights of prayer, where the people of God stay in the sanctuary agonizing all night in prayer until their tears stain the carpet and they lay hold of the horns of the altar! Why is there so much apathy and lack of personal witness among the members to the lost in the community? The answer is obvious—we need REVIVAL.

CHAPTER SEVENTEEN
THE MYTHS OF REVIVAL

"Please stop talking about Finney's 100,000 converts in Rochester, NY during the Second Great Awakening. It is merely a myth that never happened. Even Finney states it never occurred."

E. A. Johnston

As a revival scholar, it is important to distinguish the 'myths' of revival from the actual historical facts. If you continually repeat an untruth enough times it becomes a fact—even legendary! The fantastic story about Charles Finney's 100,000 converts in Rochester, NY is just a fable repeated by uniformed individuals, parroting what they have heard from others, while remaining ignorant of the real historical facts.

It began with a biographer who mistook the statement of Lyman Beecher (a well-known pastor of the Second Great Awakening) who was describing what he believed was the result of the conversions which occurred from the Second Great Awakening. Beecher in a previous paragraph mentioned Charles

Finney, but then went on to refer to the "entire amount of converts" from the Second Great Awakening as 100,000. Somehow, through human error, this fable has been passed down and repeated time and time again that Charles Grandison Finney was such a powerful influence as a preacher that he had 100,000 converts during visit to Rochester, NY.

I have known hundreds and hundreds of preachers and pastors and evangelists during my long life and I can only name personally three or five men (including myself) who have actually read Finney's Memoirs—which is a 700 page book. It is important to become a student of revival and revival history to be able to separate the fact from the fiction.

This fantastic story of "Finney's 100,000" gained ground under the preaching of Leonard Ravenhill who often mentioned it. Ravenhill was a sincere man and a wonderful preacher of revival but he was entirely out of touch of the facts of Finney in Rochester, NY. In reformed churches over the last sixty years, Rolfe Barnard unfortunately repeated the same story. Thus, it is now a so-called fact of history…but it never happened.

Charles Grandison Finney preached in Rochester, NY on two occasions: once in

1831, and again in 1842. Rochester, NY in 1831 had a population of 9,800 residents and was largely a rural area with no railroad service. How in the world can 100,000 converts magically appear from the entire population of 9,800? They cannot. It is mathematically impossible. A 100,000 persons plus their horses and buggy's could not have even fit in the town of Rochester, NY in 1831!

This takes us to Rochester, NY in 1842, eleven years later when Finney visited the town again to preach. From 1831 to 1842 the population of Rochester, NY had grown from 9,800 to a little over 20,000. How does one get 100,000 converts out of a population of 20,000? Again, it is mathematically impossible.

The reality is (taken from Finney's own reports in his memoirs) that Finney placed his number of converts in Rochester at around 800 to 1,000. That's a far cry from 100,000. But many Baptists are fascinated by numbers and numerical success in evangelism so they love to talk about Finney's 100,000. Let's look at the facts of the history of Charles Finney's time in Rochester, in 1831 where he labored for six months and preached ninety-eight sermons.

"Out of a population of about 10,000 in 1831, there were thought to be 800 converts."[13]

When I was conducting my research on my definitive biography of Asahel Nettleton, the leader of the Second Great Awakening, I traveled extensively through four States and visited over sixty locations where God moved in churches under the mighty preaching of Asahel Nettleton. Bennet Tyler, who was Nettleton's colleague and close friend estimated the number of converts under Nettleton's itinerant ministry was around 30,000. That is not one meeting but the result of a lifetime of preaching. Please stop talking about Finney's 100,000, even though it sounds better than 800.

---

[13] Charles Finney, "Memoirs", (Grand Rapids: Academie Books, 1989). p 318.

CHAPTER EIGHTEEN
SUGGESTED BOOKS ON REVIVAL

"Becoming a student of revival will help you to better pray and preach for revival. Read as many books as you can on its subject."

E. A. Johnston

My personal library has been largely full of books on revival. I have read every one of them over and over again. I am blessed every time I read a good book on revival. The following suggested reading list is by no means a comprehensive list of the best books on revival published. They are just my personal favorites which I hope will be a blessing to you as well. The important thing is to read and study about historical revivals as much as you can. The following are not in alphabetical order or even order of prominence and preference. They are just listed as is. I do highly recommend obtaining a copy of Richard Owen Roberts "An Annotated Bibliography Of Revival Literature". It will help you immensely as you build your library on revival books.

1. The Memoirs of Charles Finney, compiled by Rosell & Dupuis. Academie Books, 1989.

2. In The Day Of Thy Power, by Arthur Wallis. CLC Publications, 2010.

3. The Journals Of George Whitefield, George Whitefield, Banner of Truth, 1986.

4. 50 Years On The Battle Front With Christ, A Biography of Mordecai Ham, by Edward E. Ham, Bible & Literature Foundation, 2005.

5. Revival, by Martyn Llloyd-Jones, Crossway Books, 1987.

6. Fire In The Church, by Ted Rendall, Moody Press, 1974

7. Heart Cry For Revival, by Stephen Olford, Christian Focus, 2015.

8. Revival by Richard Owen Roberts, Tyndale House Publishers, 1982.

9. The Life And Diary Of David Brainerd, Edited by Jonathan Edwards, Baker Books, 1989

10. The Journal Once Lost, Diary of John Sung, by Levi, Genesis Books, 2008

11. A Definitive Biography of George Whitefield, Two Volumes in One, paperback, by E. A. Johnston, Old Paths Publications, 2023

12. Asahel Nettleton A Biography, Revival Preacher, Paperback, Old Paths Publications, 2023.

13. Sam Jones A New Biography, E. A. Johnston, Old Paths Publications 2023.

14. Rolfe Barnard Biography, Hitchhike Evangelist, E. A. Johnston, Old Paths Publications, 2023

15.   Sermons For Revival, E. A. Johnston, Old Paths Publications, 2023

16.   Revival Trilogy, E. A. Johnston, Old Paths Publications, 2024

17.   J. Sidlow Baxter Biography, A Heart Awake, paperback, E. A. Johnston Old Paths Publications, 2023.

ABOUT THE AUTHOR

E.A. Johnston in the Outdoor pulpit at Hanham Mount where George Whitefield preached, courtesy of Digby James.

E. A. Johnston, Ph.D., D. B. S., is a Fellow with the Stephen Olford Institute for Biblical Preaching, and is an evangelist and author with eighteen published books. He is the founder of Evangelism Awakening, a revival- based ministry whose focus is the study of historical revival, and preaching for revival in our day. He has over two thousand sermons on SermonAudio.com.

BOOKS BY E. A. JOHNSTON

1. "A Heart Awake: The Authorized Biography of J. Sidlow Baxter" Foreword by Adrian Rogers (Baker Books, Grand Rapids; 2005).

2. "Realities Of Revival" Foreword by Stephen F. Olford (Gospel Folio Press, Canada; 2005).

3. "No Turning Back" (Gospel Folio Press, Canada; 2005).

4. "The Master's Plan: Unfolding God's Blueprint For Your Life" (Gospel Folio Press, Canada; 2006).

5. "Know The Book: Bible Survey At A Glance" (Gospel Folio Press, Canada; 2007).

6. "Jua Kitabu: Tazamo la Biblia" Know The Book translated into the Swahili by missionary G. I. Harlow (Everyday Publications, Canada; 2007).

7. "Walking With God" Foreword by Ted S. Rendall (Gospel Folio Press, Canada; 2007).

8. "Return To Me: Entering A Right Relationship With God" (Gospel Folio Press, Canada; 2007).

9. "Are You In The Book Of Life?" (Gospel Folio Press, Canada; 2008).

10. "Call To Revival" Foreword By Colin Peckham (Gospel Folio Press, Canada; 2008).

11. "The Church In Revival" Foreword By Richard Owen Roberts (Gospel Folio Press, Canada; 2008).

12. "Olford On Scroggie: Stephen Olford's Notes on the Sermon Outlines of Graham Scroggie" Co-authored with Stephen Olford (Gospel Folio Press, Canada; 2008).

13. "George Whitefield A Definitive Biography In Two Volumes" (British Edition published by Tentmaker Publications, United Kingdom; 2008).

14. "George Whitefield A Definitive Biography In Two Volumes" (American edition published by Revival Literature, Asheville; 2012).

15. "God's Hitchhike Evangelist The Biography Of Rolfe Barnard" Foreword By Bob Doom (Revival Literature, Asheville; 2012).

16. "Asahel Nettleton Revival Preacher" Foreword By John Thornbury, Preface By Richard Owen Roberts (Revival Literature, Asheville; 2012).

17. "Sermons For Revival" (Revival Literature, Asheville; 2013).

18. "A Noble Company Biographical Essays on Notable Particular Baptists in America Volume 11: Portrait of Rolfe Barnard" (Particular Baptist Press, Springfield; 2018).